THE ORCHARD MASON BEE
(Osmia Lignaria Propinqua Cresson)

THE LIFE HISTORY-BIOLOGY-PROPAGATION AND USE OF A TRULY BENEVOLENT AND BENEFICIAL INSECT

by
BRIAN L. GRIFFIN

***

Illustrated by
SHARON SMITH

1st Edition
1993

Knox Cellars Publishing, Bellingham, WA

Printed in the United States of America

ISBN: 0-9635841-1-1

Typography and layout by:
  Southside Computer Services, Bellingham, WA 98225-7501

ACKNOWLEDGMENTS

The author expresses his gratitude to the following :

Dr. Philip F. Torchio, of the U.S.D.A. Bee Biology Laboratory, Utah State University, for his generosity in supplying invaluable technical information. He unselfishly supplied copies of numerous scientific papers written by himself and others, describing studies of *Osmia Lignaria.* He responded to numerous questions from the author in personal correspondence, and finally he graciously agreed to edit the final draft of this book for errors of fact.

Beverly Johanson, a good friend and English teacher, who read through several drafts, offering invaluable suggestions, criticisms, and corrections.

My cousin, and friend, Marc Miller, who sent to me the Washington State University Extension Service Bulletin which introduced me to the Orchard Mason Bee. His enthusiastic interest in my bee projects is appreciated.

Marya Griffin, my wife and gardening partner, for her support and forbearance of the time and energy that my bee activities have consumed.

DEDICATION

To my parents,

Earle and Alma Griffin,

who throughout their lives have encouraged
by example and deed my active interest in the
natural world. To both of them, now close
approaching the ninth decade of their lives,
I dedicate this little book.

TABLE OF CONTENTS

TABLE OF ILLUSTRATIONS

PREFACE

For many springs, I had seen them, small black insects feeding on my flowering shrubs. Sometimes I wondered what they were. Mostly I gave them little notice and soon forgot about them. As the blossom time passed they were forgotten until they reappeared the next spring.

Then one year I planted a Belgian Fence, a long fruit fence, consisting of forty trees, twenty varieties of apples and pears. The problems of urban pollination soon made themselves known.

The fruit trees grew nicely; each spring they burst forth with more and more blossoms, but the fruit yield was always disappointing. There simply were not enough honey bees working on those cold spring days to pollinate the trees.

A friend, hearing of my troubles, sent me Washington State University Extension Service Bulletin #0922, "Orchard Mason Bees". A fascinating door opened for me.

I read the bulletin and immediately realized that the black insects I had seen each spring were indeed a small native population of Orchard Mason bees that had been nesting in the wooden shingle roof of our garden shed.

Following the bulletin's directions, I drilled a number of holes in a fir 4x6, hung it on the southerly wall of the garden house and watched expectantly. The very next day I began to notice little black bees going in and out of the drilled holes.

My adventure with *OSMIA LIGNARIA PROPINQUA CRESSON* had begun. Soon every hole in the wooden block was sealed with a grey mud plug. I drilled another block and hung it on the garden shed. I had eighty-five filled holes that first year. Each hole contained about five nesting cells. I had collected about five hundred bees.

The next spring the population of bees on the big Pieris Japonica (*Andromeda Japonica*) bush next to the garden house was much larger. When the apples blossomed I frequently saw my black little friends working the Belgian

1

Fence.

By the first of June that year I had 583 filled nesting holes, a 680% increase in bees. I also had a vastly improved fruit set and a fine apple crop. Each year since then the fruit harvest has been generous. The bees thrive on the garden house wall, and the offspring of my original bee population have been spreading fruitfulness in urban and rural gardens throughout the Pacific Northwest.

The bees have been so successful for our garden and so many others that I have written this little book to spread the information and know-how that I have gathered.

It is my earnest hope that you will find my story of the Orchard Mason Bee interesting. If I am successful, you will soon be out in the garage with an electric drill, preparing for next spring's blossom time. You will find this gentle little bee fun to watch, and fruitful to encourage.

If you are lucky enough to have a native population to develop as I did, this book will provide you with all you need to propagate your own pollinators. If you don't have the Orchard Mason where you live, you can order a "starter set" of bees from the author. See the last page for particulars.

Chapter 1

THE FRIENDLY POLLINATOR

Washington State University gave our little friend its name: ORCHARD MASON BEE. The true scientific name is *OSMIA LIGNARIA PROPINQUA CRESSON.* Some knowledgeable entomologists call it the Blue Orchard Bee. We will call it the Orchard Mason in our book out of respect for that extension service which first brought it to our consciousness, and because Orchard Mason nicely describes both its lifestyle and its beneficial nature.

The Orchard Mason Bee is native to the United States and Canada west of the Rocky Mountains. Its eastern cousin, *OSMIA LIGNARIA LIGNARIA SAY,* populates most of North America east of the Rockies. The cousins are virtually identical except for a different set to the female's two facial horns used in shaping the mud masonry in their nesting chambers. The western bee has horns which project horizontally from the bee's face, while the horns of the eastern bee project downward at about a forty five degree angle. Science has been unable to discover any other difference. If transported across their prehistoric mountain barrier, each subspecies does well in the other's ancestral territory.

The Orchard Mason is easily found by looking on flowering shrubs and fruit trees early in the spring. In Coastal Northwest Washington State where we live, the

Pieris Japonica (*Andromeda Japonica*) shrub is among the first plants to blossom, and is an excellent place to look for the first of the emerging bees. Many insects flock to its fragrant flowers to gather the energy they will need for their annual mission.

Our tiny friend is shiny black, about 2/3 the size of a honey bee. Like all bees, it has four wings (flies have but two). Most likely the first Orchard Mason you see will be a male. (I will explain why later). He is smaller than the female and is distinguished from her by a white hair patch on his face. The male has long antennae which sweep back in a graceful curve. The female is all black with thicker antennae about half as long as those of the male.

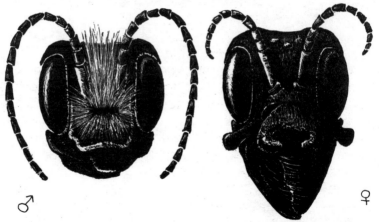

♂   ♀

The Orchard Mason is a solitary-gregarious bee. This seeming contradictory description means that while they nest in groups, if there is an adequacy of nesting holes, they are indeed solitary in nesting and propagating their species.

Honey bees, in contrast, are social insects, They depend on incredible social organization to raise, protect, feed, cool, heat and continue their species.

By comparison our Orchard Mason lives a very simple life. On the day of her emergence from the nesting cell in which she spent the winter, the female mates. She has but one day of romance, if that term applies. For the rest of her brief life she gathers food, lays eggs, packs and works mud, entirely alone, getting no help from males, or her sisters who are all busy with their own labors.

The males patrol nesting sites looking for emerging females to bestow their masculine attentions upon. They take frequent trips to the neighborhood blossoms, but only for sustenance to keep their energies at full power. Their lives are even shorter than those of the females. When they have done nature's bidding, impregnating the females, they quickly die, leaving the females to work away at the continuation of the species.

Osmia Lignaria belongs to the insect order *Hymenoptera* which includes the ants, bees and wasps. To further isolate its classification, it belongs to the Family *Megachilidae*, which in Latin means thick-jawed bees. Of course, we have already reported its genus, *Osmia,* its species, *Lignaria,* and its subspecies, *Propinqua.*

All of the Megachilids are considered long-tongued bees (better to collect nectar from flowers). The Orchard Mason will nest only in pre-existing holes. It prefers holes in wood; however, it will use holes in other materials. In the wild it searches the forests and brush patches for an unused beetle hole in a dead snag, or a broken hollow stem of a woody plant. Only when it finds the proper sized hole, will it be able to reproduce.

This specialization has no doubt limited their numbers dramatically. When compared to the adaptable honey bee, which is able to build its complex society in the walls of a house, a hollow tree, or an old box discarded by man, our Orchard Mason seems rather primitive and simple.

On the other hand, the specialized nature of the Orchard Mason results in some of the attributes that make it such a perfect urban pollinator.

First and foremost, it is entirely non-aggressive. It simply will not attack either singly or en-masse. I theorize that their solitary lifestyle is the explanation for their good nature. The Orchard Mason, unlike the honey bee, has nothing much to protect. In the natural setting she lays her eggs in an unused beetle hole in one part of the forest, then flies elsewhere to find another hole. Survival of her species depends on dispersal of the eggs rather than defense of the queen and castle, as with the honey bee.

You can be confident that the Orchard Masons are perfectly behaved guests in your garden. You and your neighbors won't even know they are around unless you stand watching by the nesting blocks. Often I stand in the busy flight pattern in front of my nesting blocks while dozens of bees pass my head. They are busily going and coming from their nesting holes and simply ignore me.

Once in a while I will move quickly and a bee, too late to change course, will bump into my head. Undaunted and without malice, she will bounce off and resume flight around me.

I am told they are capable of a mild sting; however, I have never been stung. The literature reports that the sting is about as painful as a mosquito bite. The relative toxicity of the Orchard Mason's sting has apparently not been studied. In a personal communication with Dr. Philip Torchio, at the USDA Agricultural Research Service, at Utah State University, I learned that, to his knowledge, "documentation of human reactions to bee stings has been restricted to cases involving honey bees."

He cites personal knowledge of a friend who is not reactive to honey bee stings but "is highly reactive to bumble bee stings ... others are highly reactive to wasp (hornet) stings but are not bothered by bee stings."

He goes on to remark, "we don't really know anything about human reaction to *Osmia Lignaria* stings." Surely those who are seriously allergic to insect stings and bites should be cautious in handling the Orchard Mason;

however, they can take solace from the knowledge that the bee will only sting if squeezed between the fingers or caught under clothing.

Additional comfort, Torchio says, can be taken from the fact that "these bees will not attack in numbers as do honey bees or hornets when their nests are disturbed". In fact, in my experience the Orchard Mason will not attack at all, no matter how much you agitate her nesting block. Only the female can sting. The male is entirely harmless.

A further benefit humans derive from the specialized life-style of the Orchard Mason is the ease of propagating this highly effective pollinator. All the prospective beekeeper need do to develop and keep a large pollinating population in his yard is provide the bee with holes in which to nest and blossoms from which to dine.

Remarkably, our friendly bees are also extremely efficient pollinators. Scientific studies at Utah State University have established that they are incredibly better pollinators than the honey bee.

Add to these attributes the fact that they are very easily maintained and propagated in the smallest of back yards, that they are fun and fascinating to watch, and you must conclude that Mother Nature has given us a marvelous gift to use and protect.

Chapter 2

LIFE HISTORY

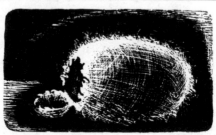

Let's begin our story of the Orchard Mason's life history in the early spring, for that is when we first see them. The weather is warming; the fruit tree buds have swollen; the very first of the garden shrubs have just started to bloom. Somewhere, inside a cocoon, deep within a hole, the bees begin to stir.

They have spent the cold winter as fully formed adults, hibernating within the confines of a waterproof insulating cocoon. They are protected by stout mud walls constructed the previous spring by their mother. Without food or liquid they have rested there in a state of torpor, using no energy, just waiting for the signal of warmth. When it comes, when the temperature rises to 50 degrees Fahrenheit for a couple of days, the bees in the wooden nesting holes awake.

The time of awakening varies from year to year depending upon the weather. The earliest bee emergence I have observed was February twenty-seventh. More typically in Western Washington, the bees emerge in late March. In colder climates emergence will be even later.

In the typical nesting hole there will be a series of nesting chambers one after the other. They are set in the holes like bullets in the tubular magazine of a rifle. In the front, in the first 70% of the nesting chambers, are the males. They awaken first and begin to chew away at the softer "nipple" end of the cocoon which almost always is pointed at the entrance hole. When he has chewed through the cocoon, the bee is confronted by a thin mud barrier. This too falls prey to his eager jaws, and now before him is another bee in some stage of awareness.

If the bee in front is a sluggard he will get a nip or two to wake him up and get him going. Sometimes the early bird behind will simply crawl over and past a slow waker.

Finally our first awaking bee confronts the thick entrance plug. This is a mud wall constructed by his mother the previous Spring. It is frequently almost 1/4 inch thick and made massively to protect the young bees from a variety of predators that would dine on them.

The entrance plug is chipped and pushed away with considerable effort, and at last our eager male bee sees daylight for the first time. He will crawl out of the hole, briefly exercise and stretch his wings, and quickly fly off, drawn by what must be a demonic hunger to a waiting blossom.

At our home a huge Pieris Japonica scrub grows 10 feet from where the nesting blocks hang on the side of the garden shed. The bee feasts on the fragrant pollen and soon returns to the area of the nesting blocks, frequently warming in the spring sunshine on the shed's shingle roof.

One after another the males struggle out of their cocoons through the debris of the now-penetrated mud walls, and emerge into the sunlight. Soon there is a veritable men's club sunning on the roof, and trading back and forth to the Pieris Japonica. They are waiting, gathering their strength for the trial before them. The male emergence lasts for ten to fifteen days depending upon the daily temperature.

Three or four days after the emergence of the males, the first female tentatively thrusts her antennae into the sunlight. She is perhaps a third larger than the patrolling males. Her antennae are short and thick and her wings appear stunted and misshapen on her back. Actually her wings are fully shaped and mature, not stunted at all. She frequently cannot fly yet, as her wings are apt to be damp from the cocoon, a condition no doubt decreed by Mother Nature to facilitate what happens next.

The female emerges from the hole and for a moment rests on the face of the nesting block. Immediately one of the waiting males lands upon her and grasps her tightly with his six legs. Frequently several other males will pile on until the virginal female loses her grip on the nesting block and the whole grasping, clutching group falls to the ground.

On the ground, in a brief mating ritual, the female is impregnated. She may be mated by several males before the day is out. After that brief day of romance, she becomes all business. Her wings dry, she takes flight, and she is no longer attractive to males nor is she interested in them.

Her only imperative now is the continuation of the species. She too flies to the Pieris Japonica to feed. Then she is off to seek a proper nesting hole. Meanwhile her ardent lover of yesterday is back on patrol, hoping for another tryst with an emerging virgin.

Approach the nesting area gingerly to avoid stepping on bees crawling on the ground. We have a concrete apron in front of the garden shed wall. There will frequently be five or six females on the ground up to ten feet from the nesting blocks. They are either being mated, or they are grooming and exercising their wings, preparing to fly.

In our garden the searching female has no problem finding a suitable nesting hole. Beside the nesting block from which the bees have emerged are several new fresh fir blocks with lots of empty 5/16 inch holes. Soon the pregnant lady and each of her sisters has found a hole to her liking and has marked it with her individual pheromone to provide a scent identity. Then she is off looking for mud, pollen and nectar with which to build and provision her nest.

The Orchard Mason does not range great distances in its search for provisions, perhaps not more than several hundred feet. Our expectant lady first finds a deposit of moist soil and collects enough to build a basal plug in her chosen hole. She then finds a source of pollen and nectar nearby. Hopefully it is the blossoms of several of the fruit trees now in bloom on the Belgian Fence. She gathers a full load of pollen, drinks in nectar, and then flies back to the hole. She regurgitates the nectar, and tamps the pollen down on top of it.

By the afternoon she has a nice little pile of food stacked up. First the nectar, then the pollen, then more nectar. Back and forth she speeds to the blossoms loading up all she can carry. Again and again she returns to the blossoms, until finally the mixture and the top coating are just right.

Now with maternal precision she turns around and backs down the hole to the waiting food provisions. She carefully positions herself over the sticky mass, and deposits a small white egg directly into the waiting pollen and nectar.

The egg, three millimeters long, is shaped like a wiener sausage with a wiener-like curve. One end is embedded in the food mass so that the egg sticks out erect. It almost shimmers with a translucent sort of glow. We will leave the egg for a bit and continue with its story later. Now we must follow the proud mother as she speeds out of the hole to the mud quarry.

The egg must be immediately protected and another nesting chamber prepared for a brother or sister. The female flies off to a place on the ground where the proper dirt or clay exists. Moisture is important because our

mother-to-be must now become a mason. Finding soil of the proper moisture content, she rolls up a ball of mud mortar and, grasping it in her mandibles, flies back to the hole and her exposed egg. She attaches her mortar to the wall of the hole and returns for more.

By the end of the day she has completed the cell. She has constructed a circular wall which seals off the nesting chamber almost like a rigid diaphragm. The egg is safe for now. It is late in the afternoon and our hard working lady is getting cold. She will stay in the nesting hole during the evening. It has become home. Meanwhile, within her another egg is maturing.

And so it goes for the next thirty or so days. She will begin work when the temperature rises to about fifty-five degrees Fahrenheit; she will cease when the temperature falls below that or the sun goes down. She will lay about thirty-five eggs in her brief life. Then she will die, her life's work left behind in a series of holes that she has found.

By the first week of June all of her contemporaries will also have died. There will not be an Orchard Mason bee to be seen.

Elsewhere life goes on. Back in the nesting chambers spread through the forest or concentrated in hundreds of holes in the wooden blocks in our garden, the eggs are hatching. Actually hatching is not the proper word. Bird eggs hatch, with a dramatic rending of their shell, to reveal a complete, if immature, chick. Bee eggs evolve with far less drama.

Three to four days after it is laid, the egg begins the first of a long chain of transformations from egg, to a tiny larva that looks pretty much like the original egg, except that now it lies flat on the food provision. The larva hardly moves. It slowly descends to lie on the food provision with its eating end attached to the food with small mouth parts.

The hungry larva eats and eats. Over a period of 28-29 days the food pile gets smaller and the larva gets larger. Finally the food is gone. During all but the last few days of this process the observer sees very little movement of the larva. It has simply been a great fat tubular lump ingesting all that rich food left behind by mama.

In the last few days it begins to defecate. Soon one can see small dark brown granule-like feces which begin to collect at one end of the nesting chamber.

When the food has been consumed there is a cessation of activity. Then, after several days of rest, the larva gets rather active. Its anterior begins to revolve in a circular motion, frequently touching the sides of the cell wall as though sticking something up there. Around and around goes the south end of the fat white larva, and finally after several hours the larva is seen less clearly.

The observer begins to think his sight is failing as the larva slowly fades from view behind the thin veil it is spinning. It is slowly weaving a cocoon about itself with invisible thread.

When I first observed the weaving, I noticed the faint veil effect in the evening before retiring. When I awoke eight hours later, the larva had disappeared and in its place was an opaque, pinkish- white cocoon. A small miracle had taken place overnight.

The cocoon slowly turns color until in a few days it is a rather dark Chesapeake retriever brown. It will have a few fecal granules woven into the outside layer, and it will be very tough. Its interior is varnished with a waterproof substance. It is surprisingly resistant to cutting, even with sharp scissors. Clearly the cocoon is an effective, strong, and, I presume, well-insulated home for the long, cold winter ahead.

After what must have been a Herculean effort in spinning the cocoon, the larva enters a month-long period of inactivity, apparently resting from its labors. Then it changes into a pupa. In the pupal stage our bee-to-be

begins to show some of its final shape. It rather looks like an insect mummy with many of the body parts now apparent but encased tightly in the pupal case.

Within the case great changes are occurring. After several weeks the final molt occurs and a complete imago, or adult bee, rests within the protective confines of the cocoon. It began in March or April - all through the summer the changes continued - and now it is September and the metamorphosis is complete.

The now-adult bee lies in its cocoon ready to go. However, Mother Nature in her wisdom is not ready for our little friend yet. If it is nature's intent that the Orchard Mason be her pollinator; in September there is nothing to pollinate. The bee must sleep through the winter and emerge in the spring with the blossoms. And so it happens. Through the cold winter the bees lie in their insulated cocoons, further insulated by wood, protected from predators by the mud walls erected by their mother. There they lie until spring when they awake to undertake their crucial role in the balance of nature: pollination.

The life history of the Orchard Mason is only one of nature's small miracles. Nevertheless its intricate balance and incredible practicality fill me with awe. If you share my fascination to this point, perhaps you will also enjoy some of the small facts about this life story:

* * *

The female, when laying eggs, is able to determine the sex of the egg she is laying. She intentionally lays female eggs first, in the back cells of a long nesting hole. Production of female progeny is most important in continuing the species, and are thus best protected from predators. The hapless males occupying the front chambers are sacrificed to any invaders, hopefully satisfying them, or at least slowing them down until the females can escape in the spring. It only takes one male to impregnate many females. On average two thirds of the eggs laid are males.

They are effective sacrifices to divert the enemy at the gate.

*   *   *

More than ninety percent of the females emerge in a two hour period in the morning, from 9:00 A.M. to 11:00. At this time the ambient temperature is low and humidity levels are high. It is postulated that large quantities of the female attractant pheromone are released during this time, and that the dissipation rate of the attractant is reduced because of the lower temperature and higher humidity; thus the odds are improved that the males will find the females and that they will do their best to propagate the race.

*   *   *

The females gather wet soil to build the masonry walls of the nesting cells. The soil must be of just the right moisture content. To get the correct mixture the bees will excavate a "mine", digging down to the proper moisture content.

*   *   *

Each cell partition takes eight to twelve mud collecting trips. Provisioning each cell with the pollen and nectar required takes fourteen to thirty-five foraging trips.

*   *   *

In the cell the female kneads the mud to an even consistency with her mandibles. She then applies the mud by pressing it with her revolving body, finishing and polishing the masonry with the horns on her head.

*   *   *

The Orchard Mason will not excavate a nesting hole. Its survival as a species depends on finding holes made by other creatures. In the wild, beetle holes in dead or dying timber are major nesting sites. I have found the bees nesting in driftwood logs by the sea shore. They occupy the tunnels dug by the marine Teredos, commonly called pile worms.

Chapter 3

POLLINATION

If you believe nature has a purpose for all earth's creatures, then you have to believe that the Orchard Mason Bee was put on this earth to pollinate.

Let's discuss for a minute the pollination of an ordinary backyard apple. If you remember your high school biology, you know that the apple blossom has a number of stamen. At the tip of the stamen is the pollen-bearing anther. In the center of the blossom are the styles, at the tips of which are the five stigmas. Each style has a hollow passageway that leads down into the blossom to the ovaries.

Pollen from the anthers of one apple cultivar must somehow find its way to the stigmatic surfaces of compatible but different apple cultivars during the short period of stigma receptivity. To make things more difficult, at least two pollen granules must enter each stigma for successful pollination. The pollen travels down the tube in the stigma to the ovary where fertilization takes place.

If several of the stigmas fail to receive the required pollen, their connected ovaries will not develop seeds and that apple will be lopsided and not marketable. If pollen from a compatible apple fails to find its way to our blossom there will be no fruit at all.

The transfer of pollen from blossom to blossom occurs in many ways. Wind and air currents accomplish some of it.

Insects of many kinds contribute to the job.   Flies, butterflies, and moths, including the nocturnal species, all help. The best of the pollinators, however, are the bees. The widely used honey bees are the great commercial pollinators of the world because they exist in incredible numbers, are highly transportable and have social habits that man has adapted to his use for thousands of years.

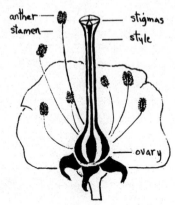

Perhaps the best proof of their symbiotic relationship with man is the fact that they are not native to North America. The honey bee was brought to this continent by the earliest colonists sometime before 1638.

Prior to the arrival of the honey bee, the native fruits and flowers of North America were obviously being successfully pollinated. The best of the native pollinators were the estimated 3500 species of wild bees that still inhabit North America. The vast majority of those bees are solitary bees just like our Orchard Mason.

Pollination by native bees still plays a massive and important role in the life cycles of not only native plants but of our commercial agricultural crops as well. Many of these wild bees are much better pollinators of specific plants than the honey bee. Studies by USDA/ARS researchers at Utah State University have established that the Orchard Mason, bee for bee, is far more efficient as a pollinator of apples, pears, cherries and almonds than the honey bee. "How can that be?", you ask. The answer lies in both bee biology and differences in life style.

Remember watching the honey bee in your garden? She flies from blossom to blossom, carefully plucking pollen granules and stuffing them in the tiny "pollen baskets" on her legs.

This efficient and tidy method of carrying pollen does

not aid in pollination. It is too neat and clean. The pollen does not fall from her "pollen basket", thus it cannot pollinate. Most of her pollination is done by spilled pollen granules that have accidentally caught on her body hairs.

Our Orchard Mason is not as sophisticated as the honey bee. She has no leg pockets at all. She must carry pollen by wedging the granules into several rows of stiff specialized hairs on her abdomen called scopa. They do a good job of carrying pollen, but some falls out as the bee tries to stuff more and more into this primitive cargo rack. It is kind of like stuffing rice grains into a hair brush - it carries plenty but spills a lot also. She is dragging her scopa over every blossom she visits, and she visits plenty.

The Orchard Mason holds another advantage in the pollination derby. She is much hairier on the lower sections of her body than the honey bee. Consequently she carries around more pollen caught in her body hair. As she crawls over the blossoms she redistributes much of this pollen, some of it to the stigma of a compatible fruit.

Greg Dickman, in his brochure, "Orchard Bees", states that the Orchard Mason visits more blossoms each day than the honey bee, and pollinates a much higher percentage of those blooms visited. He states that the honey bee visits an average seven hundred blooms daily. It pollinates only thirty of them, a mere five percent success rate. He further claims that our Orchard Mason pollinates 1600 flowers per day, a pollination success rate of ninety-five to ninety-nine percent.   Philip Torchio, at USDA/ARS, Utah State, questions the validity of Dickman's numbers, suggesting that the definitive study has not been done.

It remains clear however, that the Orchard Mason is a far better pollinator of early fruits and nuts, than the honey bee.   This advantage results from a number of biological and behavioral features of both the bee and the blossom.

In many cultivars of apples, the blossom is so shaped that the honey bee, foraging for nectar, lands on the blossom petal and never touches the anther which bears the pollen. The Orchard Mason of both sexes always lands on the sexual column of any apple flower.

The Orchard Mason flits nervously from tree to tree as it forages. In contrast, the honey bee will spend a lot of time on one tree, going from blossom to blossom in a small area on that tree. As most apples require cross pollination, the Orchard Mason's nervous habits make it far more likely to transfer pollen from one tree species to another.   The essential cross- pollination is achieved because the Orchard Mason has visited many trees while the honey bee diligently filled her pollen bags from but one tree.

A further advantage stems from the fact that the Orchard Mason initiates daily flight at a temperature of thirteen degrees centigrade, or fifty-five degrees Fahrenheit: just the temperature at which apple pollen begins germination. The honey bee, guided by its southern European genes, begins flight at a little warmer temperature and so misses some time at work on early spring mornings. Conversely, any insect operating at temperatures colder than the germination temperature of apple pollen will not be effective as a pollinator. The Orchard Mason fits the apple very nicely. Studies demonstrate that maximum pollination in a commercial apple orchard can be achieved with as few as 250 female Orchard Masons per acre. Compare that with the standard orchardist's practice of providing one honey bee hive for each two acres of orchard. A hive is apt to contain 40,000 bees, a large percentage of which are foragers.

Faced with the evidence of the Orchard Mason's superiority as a pollinator, one is quick to ask, "Why aren't there more of them and why are they not used commercially?"

The first part of the question is answered by the fact that the Orchard Mason is a solitary bee; their reproduction opportunities are limited, unlike the highly organized social bees, such as the honey bee and bumble bee, or the social wasps, Hornets and Yellow Jackets. Our friendly Orchard Mason does not make a nest; she must find a hole ready made for her. If you think about it, holes of the proper nesting diameter are hard to find in nature. That fact alone limits the population.

Furthermore, each female Orchard Mason can only lay about thirty-five eggs in her brief life span. Contrast that with the incredible offspring production of the honey bee hive which can produce 30,000 bees in a season.

And why are they not used commercially? There may well be a commercial use for our efficient friend. Dr. Philip Torchio has been studying this possibility for some time. It now appears that when done properly the Orchard Mason can be transported successfully from orchard to orchard. I will be conducting a trial experiment in the spring of 1993 in a western Washington apple orchard to explore the commercial possibilities.

One clear limitation of the Orchard Mason is that it can only be used to pollinate early spring crops. Unlike the honey bee which operates all summer and into the fall, the Orchard Mason is dead by the first of June.

Its propagation to commercially viable populations requires some cost of labor and materials, but that is also true of the honey bee. Commercial use of the Orchard Mason may well be viable in the future, but more must be learned about this marvelous insect and its commercial potential.

Chapter 4

SIMILAR SPECIES

The Orchard Mason Bee *(Osmia Lignaria Propinqua Cresson)* is not the only solitary bee pollinating our world. In fact there may be 30,000 species of solitary bees on this planet. They represent 99 percent of all bee species and are more numerous than all the earth's birds and mammals combined.

Their diversity is incredible. The smallest are no more than two millimeters in length and the largest approach eighty millimeters. Some nest only in existing holes, while some drill their own nesting tunnels in wood or earth. Some are nocturnal, others fly only at dawn or dusk. Some bees, like the Orchard Mason, have a wide distribution over huge areas. Some bee species are specific to a particular township.

These non-honey bees have complicated biologies. In most the adult form is short lived, their nesting sites are often difficult to locate, some produce offspring only every other year, and they are usually small in population and very easy to overlook.

In terms of biomass, the total weight of all the individuals of one species on the earth, the honey bees probably surpass all of the solitary bees put together. The highly successful social insects such as honey bees, ants, and termites, together comprise a huge percentage of insect biomass and, for that matter, the earth's biomass.

Edward O. Wilson, a world authority on ants, says in an essay for the Xerces Society magazine, Wings, "The ants and termites, the most highly social of all organisms, plus the social wasps and social bees which rival them in colonial organization, make up about eighty percent of the biomass."

That incredible statement is a clear illustration of the advantages of social organization. The earth's biomass includes the combined body weight of every man, animal, reptile, fish, and insect. Just think of it: every thing on earth that walks, crawls, swims, flies or slithers. Eighty percent of that combined weight is attributed to the social insects.

The social insects comprise a tiny percentage of the number of species, but a huge percentage of the number of individuals. Who says it doesn't pay to be organized?

The Orchard Mason Bee has competitors vying for it's nesting sites and food supply. In most cases the competitors' geographical spread is not as large as the Orchard Masons', or they are foreign immigrants which have not established themselves in your area. Depending upon where you live, your Orchard Masons may be coexisting with some of the bees described in this chapter.

You may wish to identify and propagate some of these alternative bees to fit your own interests and goals. You will recall that we have discussed the two sub-species of *OSMIA LIGNARIA*, *Osmia Lignaria Propinqua Cresson* and its eastern cousin, *Osmia Lignaria Lignaria Say*. Now let's meet:

OSMIA CALIFORNICA CRESSON
A leaf cutting bee that emerges about the time the Orchard Mason is at its peak of activity. This bee competes with the Orchard Mason for nesting holes. It is mainly a pollinator of plants in the family *Compositae*.

This bee has a similar lifestyle except that it does not use mud to construct its nesting cells. It uses a composite pulp made of macerated leaf and soil. Pieces are cut from the leaves of specific plants, chewed into a pulp ball which is then rolled in soil until coated. The leaf-soil ball is then carried to the nest hole where it is further processed by chewing until it becomes the desired consistency to make the cell division walls. The composite mixture is strengthened with a coating of nectar that hardens as it dries.

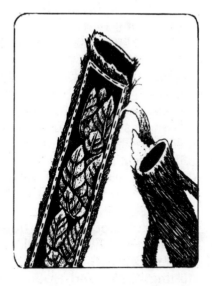

The offspring of *Osmia Californica* may spend either one or two winters in the nesting cell. One generation of the bee can emerge over a two year period, some offspring maturing this year and some the next. This seemingly random maturation process is called parsivoltinism.

OSMIA MONTANA MONTANA CRESSON

This bee also competes with the Orchard Mason for nesting holes where their ranges overlap. Another leaf cutter, this bee emerges 1-2 weeks after *O. Californica*. It constructs its nesting cells with pure leaf pulp which is not mixed with soil. This bee is also parsivoltine. Sometimes overwintering larvae and overwintering adults are found in adjacent cells in the same nesting hole. If the larvae, destined to spend two winters in the cell, happen to be in the forward cells, their adult brothers or sisters will destroy them as they struggle to emerge in an earlier spring.

NOMIA MELANDERI (ALKALI BEE)

A bee of the western deserts, this bee is an effective pollinator of alfalfa when the crop is bordered by alkali flats where the bee nests. The alkali bee is about 2/3 the size of the honey bee and is identified by gold to turquoise abdominal stripes. It nests in large populations in the soil of alkali flats. Each nest has a main burrow leading from the entrance hole to a carved out chamber twelve to sixty centimeters below the soil surface. A cluster of six to twenty-two elongate cells are constructed below the chamber and each is oriented vertically. Each cell is coated with a waterproofing secretion.

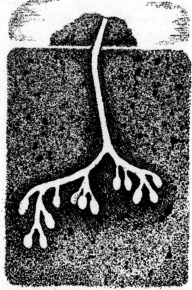

The alkali bee provisions its cells with nectar and pollen and lays a single egg in each. The cell is then capped with a soil plug. The larva overwinters, pupates in the spring, and the adult alkali bee digs out of the soil in May or June to repeat the cycle.

The alkali bee visits a wide variety of flowering plants including alfalfa, clover, onion and mint crops. It has been a valuable pollinator of commercial crops for many years. Its nesting sites have been successfully replicated and managed so that this bee remains a valuable agricultural pollinator in its range.

MEGACHILE ROTUNDATA (ALFALFA LEAFCUTTING BEE)

This is a Eurasian bee that was accidentally introduced on the east coast of North America in the early 1930's. It apparently first became established near Washington D.C. and rapidly migrated across the continent where it reached the Pacific Northwest sometime prior to the 1950s.

Soon afterwards, alfalfa seed growers in Utah and Idaho began noticing the bee visiting the bloom in their fields. Subsequent studies of this newcomer established its unique value in alfalfa pollination and a viable way to propagate and transport this bee. The entire West is now the beneficiary of this successful bee, and it has been reintroduced to Europe and other parts of the world as the dominant pollinator of alfalfa.

This bee is about half the size of the honey bee, its abdomen striped with bands of light colored hair. It carries pollen in its scopa as does *Osmia Lignaria*. It nests in existing holes and constructs its cell partitions by overlapping circular sections of leaf that it cuts. The pieces are purposely overlapped, the edges chewed and tamped into place. The chewed areas of leaf dry and form strong bonding lines interconnecting the overlapped leaf pieces. The result is a bullet-shaped leaf cell.

Pollen and nectar are gathered, deposited in the cell, and a single egg is laid in the deposit. The female then seals the cell with circular leaf pieces chewed and tamped into place. She then begins another cell immediately on top of the first.

Modern propagation of this valuable bee involves large nesting boards with drilled holes set in the alfalfa fields. A drive through western alfalfa country will reveal these nesting boards, looking for all the world like sign boards standing in the flat fields.

OSMIA CORNIFRONS (HORNED-FACED BEE)

This small orange striped bee is a native of Japan. At one time it was being distributed by the U.S. Department of Agriculture, which had concluded that the bee had valuable commercial potential.

O. Cornifrons has long been used for fruit pollination in Japan where it is cultivated extensively. It has shown some difficulty in surviving severe winters in North America, but has been successfully established in a number of areas.

It competes with Orchard Masons for nesting sites. Because it is about two thirds the size of the Orchard

Mason, it can utilize smaller nesting holes, but is quite happy with a 5/16 inch hole favored by the Orchard Mason. The author knows of a bee fancier in the Pacific Northwest who introduced *Cornifrons* into his urban lot. They share the same nesting blocks with Orchard Masons and he can no longer keep them separate. They coexist nicely.

OSMIA COERULESCENS

This bee is a species native to Europe. It is abundant throughout France and Spain, and was introduced accidentally into the United States. It is found in localized areas east of the Rocky Mountains. It is apparently an effective pollinator of red clover but has not been developed commercially.

OSMIA SANRAFAELAE

This is a species restricted to the San Rafael Desert in Southern Utah. It's an effective pollinator of alfalfa, and will nest in man- made nesting materials.

As you can see, the Orchard Mason Bee is not the only choice for the back yard fruit grower who wishes to improve pollination. It does appear to this writer, however, that the Orchard Mason might be the best choice. It apparently is tolerant of a wider range of climactic conditions, and because it favors fruit blossoms but will utilize many other flowers and even dandelions, it will prosper where more specialized bees would not.

The geographic range of the Orchard Mason is so widespread and general that it is entirely possible that you, the reader, have the Orchard Mason in your yard already. If so, the following chapter on propagation will contain all that you need to know to establish your own population of these efficient pollinators.

Chapter 5

PROPAGATION

You have read about the fascinating life history of the Orchard Mason Bee. Now all you need to do to develop a healthy population of bees to pollinate your own fruits and flowers is use that knowledge in a practical way.

First you must locate a native population of bees. Remember that our friend is native to every state west of the Rockies, and his close cousin lives in most of the states east of the Rockies. If you are very lucky, you may have them in your back yard right now. You may never have seen them, but then, you didn't know what to look for previously, did you? Look for the bees on the earliest spring blossoms. Look in your own yard. Take long walks perusing the neighborhood shrubs, and be sure to wander in your city parks, rural woodlands, or wherever you see new blossoms, for there you will find the Orchard Mason.

If you have them, or know where a population is, all you need do is drill 5/16 inch holes in a block of wood to create a nesting trap. Hang the trap at the populated site at the end of February or whenever the weather begins to warm, and wait. By the first of June, you will have a block full of bee eggs that you can carefully bring home.

If you are not lucky enough to find bees your first Spring, or if you wish to be sure to get a start, you may want to buy bees. See the last page in the book for particulars.

Let's assume that you have a few bees using your yard. The challenge then is to create an environment in which they can prosper and multiply. Like any of God's creatures, our winged friends need ample food, shelter in which to nest, and finally, an environment which at the very least does not kill them.

The food that sustains the Orchard Mason Bee is, of course, pollen and nectar from the flowers of trees and plants. The Orchard Mason, unlike some of the wild bees, is not a very fussy feeder. It will use the blossoms of a wide range of plants for its sustenance. I have observed the bees on dandelions, shrubs of all kinds, and most importantly, on fruit trees.

It is vital that your location have not only a good supply of blossoms, but a supply of blossoms over the entire period that the bees are foraging. In the Pacific Northwest that period is roughly from March 15th to June 1st. Of course, the bee's emergence depends on the weather, but you can count on nature to time their emergence with the appearance of the first blossoms.

Optimum bee propagation requires that you have more than just fruit blossoms to feed your bees. The fruit tree blossom period is short. Most fruit varieties bloom and wither in little more than a week. If you had but one variety of fruit in your yard, and no other blooms of any kind, your poor bees would eat and lay eggs for only the week that your fruit blossomed.

They would have no choice but to leave your yard for a location with a food supply of longer duration. The eggs they had laid in your nests would be perfectly good. It is just that you would be getting but seven or eight nesting cells from each female that you released. Your carefully nurtured females would be laying another 25 eggs or so in someone else's garden. In order to increase your bee population and keep them for the long term, you must plant for variety and sustained pollen yield.

I heartily recommend that you plant the Pieris Japonica shrub if it will thrive in your climate. This large evergreen shrub does very well in the wet parts of the Pacific Northwest where I live. The Sunset Garden Book shows it  as "Pieris Japonica (*Andromeda japonica*)." Its chief feature is cascades of tiny bell-like blossoms that bloom very early in the spring and continue for weeks and weeks.

My bees seem to love it and feed on it all through the blossom time. Our *Andromeda japonica* stands ten feet from the bee colony, large and accessible, I think it may be an important factor in the six hundred per cent increase in bee population I enjoy most years.

Further evidence of the Pieris Japonica's attraction for the Orchard Mason is given by the remarkable number of Orchard Masons that visit a group of the shrubs planted in the landscaping of a downtown bank in my city. The bank is situated in the center of a typical asphalt and concrete downtown environment, but somewhere nearby, there is a thriving Orchard Mason colony. Each spring I am astonished by the feeding frenzy that I see on those shrubs. When loaded with pollen, our little black friends dash off across the busy city street to the west of the bank and disappear. I have tried to follow them to their home without success. Perhaps next year I will find the nesting site. It ought to be a great location to hang a few of my nesting blocks. I would like some of that city-tough strain in my breeding stock.

Osmia Lignaria does not range far in its quest for food, perhaps no further than the length of a football field in any direction. A dense urban location becomes a great advantage when this fact is considered. My bee colony is in the old section of a small city. The building lots were platted with twenty- five foot widths. While most of the houses are built on two or even three lots, the neighborhood density is very high. It is also an area of very serious gardeners. There is a wide variety of trees, shrubs and flowers within the bees' range, and consequently, my bees don't want for sources of food during their short lifetimes.

The bees must not only find pollen and nectar to feed themselves; they must find and transport the food provision for up to thirty-five nesting cells. There is a direct relationship between the abundance of food sources and the number of cells prepared and eggs laid in the life of a female. There is, further, a relationship between the food supply and the size of the offspring. One would suppose that the larger the offspring, the better they are able to cope with the trials of life and the more successful they will be in reproducing themselves.

Other factors being equal, the single most important element in developing a large Orchard Mason Bee Population is housing. The bee must have a hole of a proper size available before it can reproduce. If you wish a large number of bees you must provide a large number of holes. It is just that simple.

Remember, the Orchard Mason does not make its own nesting hole. It must find a hole, and some other creature must make the hole.

You can achieve remarkable increases in your backyard bee population simply by providing more and more nesting holes as your population grows. If you cease providing fresh holes year after year, your population must stay stable.

Let's begin with the size of the hole. We suggest that you use only a 5/16 inch or seven millimeter hole. The bee will successfully nest in both smaller or larger holes, but it will not be as successful in a size other than 5/16 inch.

I did not always believe that 5/16 inch was the proper size. Early in my experience with the Orchard Mason, I ran an experiment. I drilled a large nesting block with four different sized holes: twenty holes each of 1/4 inch, 5/16 inch, 3/8 inch, and finally huge looking 7/16 inch holes.

I hung the block in my nesting colony and was astonished to note that the bees filled every one of the 1/4 inch holes before they started on the larger holes. Their second choice was the 5/16 inch, and finally the 3/8 inch.

They never did use the 7/16 inch.

I was elated. I had made a discovery and I felt very scientific and wise. All of my nesting blocks that year were drilled with 1/4 inch holes. They filled rapidly and I had the usual good percentage of increase. I was quite self satisfied as several gardening writers were recommending 5/16 inch holes and even Washington State University seemed to give the larger hole the nod.

I had proved them wrong. Clearly, I reasoned, the bees would choose the smallest hole they could fit into simply because they would have to haul less mud to seal the nesting cells. Everyone knows that Mother Nature is efficient above all else. How could all those experts have been so wrong?

It was mid winter when I got my comeuppance. Dr. Torchio, at Utah State, sent me a paper that established that the Orchard Mason Bee lays a higher percentage of female eggs in the 5/16 inch hole than she does in the smaller 1/4 inch hole.

I was doing fine using the smaller holes, but I would have been doing better with the 5/16 inch. The rate of population increase will be improved using the larger holes. Ah, humility. What seems so obvious and logical to us mere mortals is not always so in nature's great scheme. I can find no logic to support the bee's choice of the larger hole so I have simply rationalized it by reminding myself of another advantage of the larger hole. The 5/16 inch hole is far less likely to be plugged by swelling wood fibers and thus is a better size.

A hole drilled in a soft block of wood tends to contain uncut and torn wood fibers. When that block of wood is exposed to the weather, it will pick up moisture. The wood fiber ends that were laid back by the whirling drill bit will swell and straighten and tend to plug a small hole. This swelling problem can be reduced by using a very sharp drill bit that cuts the fibers cleanly. My experience says that a "brad point" drill bit is far superior to the standard "Jobbers bit" of common usage.

Let's take a look at a variety of ways to provide nesting

sites for the Orchard Mason that we are trying to attract and propagate. I shall discuss several of the common techniques, but remember that the bee first and foremost requires a hole. You are free to use your imagination as to the presentation to the bee.

WOODEN BLOCKS

The bees prefer nesting in holes in wood over any other material. I make my nesting blocks of large four by six inch mill ends purchased from a local lumber mill. Pine, fir or hemlock work equally well. Be sure to use untreated wood.

In a four inch deep block I drill a 5/16 inch hole to within 1/2 inches of the back. I don't think there is any reason you could not drill a hole twice that deep if you had wood thick enough and a drill bit long enough. Three and one half inches works fine, however. Be sure not to drill all the way through the block - predators can get in the back door that way.

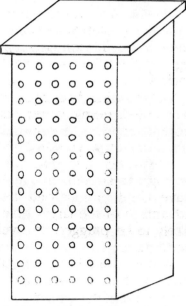

Drill the holes on 3/4 inch centers. In other words, the center of each hole should be 3/4 inch away from the center of all holes around it. I line all of my holes up in nice straight and square lines. I doubt that the bees care. I am sure that random holes drilled all over a piece of wood without rhyme nor reason would suit them just as well. I simply prefer the looks of a neatly laid out block. It also helps in counting completed holes as spring progresses, something that you will surely be doing.

Wooden blocks do have a problem with splitting. It is therefore important to select wood of as good a quality as possible, and to use dry wood. I have never painted or treated my blocks; however I have read of others doing so before drilling them. I rely on selecting good wood and a piece of cedar shingle to form a roof, keeping rain from the exposed end grain. The roof should extend out over the front of the block to keep the drip line beyond the drilled holes.

Here's a tip on drilling holes close to the edges of the blocks without splitting them. Simply clamp boards tightly on either side of the block. The inward pressure of the clamping technique will prevent split out.

I cut one end of the block at an angle tilting to the front, and tack on the little piece of cedar shingle to shed rain. Then I drill one more hole at the top center of the backside of the block. This is the hanging hole. A nail driven into the outside wall of your house or outbuilding is now all you need to begin trapping the not so wily Orchard Mason Bee. Each block has 102 holes.

The wooden blocks can be used year after year. The bees will clean the holes out so that they can be re-used You might reduce mite infestation and improve nest sanitation by putting up new nesting blocks each year, but it is surely not necessary.

Some people simply drill holes in the woodpile, or in the old dead cherry tree in the back yard. This rustic method seems to work just fine.

SODA STRAWS

The Orchard Mason may prefer to nest in wood, but she will very successfully nest in plastic or paper soda straws folded once in the center and stuck into a tin can, cardboard milk carton or any other container.

If wood is not available to you, simply buy the large sized straws. The inside dimension should be about 7 mm. Fold each one in half to seal off the back of what are now two nesting holes.

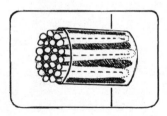

When you have folded enough of them to fill your container, bind them together with masking tape so that they will be stable and not spring free.

If possible, fashion a little roof over the front to keep the rain from the hole entrances and mount the trap in some way so that the holes lie horizontally. Use your imagination; the bees won't mind. I have seen soda straws stuck in plastic sewer pipe sections, one half gallon milk cartons, and rusting tin cans. Anything that will hold the straws and keep them dry will work. The disadvantage of soda straws is their vulnerability to depredation by the monodonto-merus wasp described in Chapter Six.

CARDBOARD TUBES

Some Orchard Mason propagators prefer to place small cardboard tubes in holes specially drilled in a block of wood.

Although I have never used this method, it does provide some interesting advantages. With this method, one can insert new tubes in a block each year. This technique is more hygienic than simply reusing a nesting block in which the bees had nested. Some problems of disease and mite depredation might be reduced. The tubes are removed each fall and stored in a spare refrigerator, assuring proper atmospheric and temperature conditions until time to reinsert them in emergence blocks. By holding the tubes up to the light you can count the number of bees in each tube, a great help if you want to sell bees, or plan to pollinate an orchard for someone else. You will know exactly how many bees you have.

Finally, if your bees are bothered by a parasite that feeds on the spare pollen in the cell, you can unpeel the windings of the tube, collect the hibernating bees in their cocoons, treat the cocoons for the parasites and then reinsert the cocoons into clean new tubes.

A piece of cotton stuffed into the tube end simulates the mud plug, and the parasite-free bees will be ready to go in the spring.

OTHER NESTING POSSIBILITIES

It is well established that the Orchard Mason reproduces in cedar shingle roofs. In fact the native population in my back yard had, for years, been nesting in the shingles of a small garden shed. If you will look carefully at a wood shingle roof, you will notice that the aperture created by two shingles laid side by side on the shingle below is often about 5/16 inch wide. When you lay the next course of shingles, the shingle on top of that aperture creates a square hole of just the right dimensions for a bee nest.

While the bees prefer a horizontal nesting hole, they will also nest in vertical shingle walls frequently found on houses. The slight pitch created by a sloping roof or a vertical hole doesn't bother them at all. In fact I have proof that they thrive in completely upside down nesting holes.

A large number of my breeding stock was trapped last year at a home in Kirkland, Washington. The following story represents the only negative report I have ever heard about the Orchard Mason Bee.

While selling bees at the Northwest Flower and Garden Show in Seattle's Convention Center, I talked with a couple who had a bee problem. They listened to my presentation. Afterward they came up to tell me that their house was infested with Orchard Mason bees.

It seemed that they had recently remodeled their older home. They had carefully covered the outside walls with cedar shingles.

In addition they had carefully placed each shingle the exact distance apart to get the proper shadow effect. You guessed it: the shingles were just 5/16 inch apart. They had created a giant nursery for Orchard Masons.

They had so many bees coming and going across their outside deck area each spring that they didn't enjoy eating out, or sitting on the deck.   They had hired a pest exterminator to spray the walls but the spray had no effect at all. Next year's bees were all safe behind those shingles and the stout mud walls of the cells. Those nesting holes were of course vertical. The bees entered from below.

There is a happy ending to the story. I offered my assistance and set my fir trap blocks all about their deck. The blocks contained two thousand 5/16 inch holes capable of holding about seven nesting cells each.

I was gratified to find that the bees preferred my nesting blocks to the spaces between the shingles. The majority of the bees nested in my blocks. By the end of the season in June they had filled 1830 of the holes, and I had collected approximately twelve thousand bees. At least twelve thousand fewer bees will be bothering those folks next spring. I will redistribute those bees across the country to bring their considerable benefits to home gardeners and fruit growers.

It appears that the size of the hole may be more important than the nesting material. In the urgency of reproductive fervor, our Orchard Mason will build nesting cells in strange places. I have seen a recorder, a flute-like musical instrument, with a nesting cell plugging its air passage.

A friend recently told me he discovered the reason his outdoor lights were not turning on at dusk and off at dawn this spring. He found that the short tube opening to the light-sensing device was plugged with mud. When digging it out, he was surprised to excavate sweet smelling pollen and nectar. The culprit was, of course, our friendly Orchard Mason who laid her egg in his plastic light sensor.

NESTING SITES

I have been selling nesting blocks complete with hibernating bees for several years now. It has been interesting to observe the propagation success of those blocks placed in different sites. I have developed some strong impressions about which kinds of sites work the best.

The most successful site I know of is the infested shingle house previously mentioned. It sits about 100 feet up hill from a large lake. It is surrounded by large trees although it gets lots of sun from mid morning on. The trees are native, big leafed maples, a wonderful source of spring pollen.

The site appears protected from the prevailing winds.

Our own propagation site is very successful. We generate a six hundred percent population increase in a good year. For each filled nesting block set out in the spring, we have seven filled blocks by June.

Our nesting blocks are hung on the wall of a small garden shed. The wall fronts on a now unused dog kennel. Ivy and espaliered apple trees grow on the old kennel fence, providing excellent wind protection. Just above the hanging trap nests is the small shingle roof which not only protects the blocks from rain, but provides a resting and warming surface. The shingles of this roof were the original nesting place of my colony of bees. We constantly see bees landing briefly on the roof to groom or to warm themselves in the morning.

The nesting blocks face south, but the exposure is such that the early morning sun hits them and they are in full sun until early afternoon. In the temperate Western Washington climate the bees don't seem to get too hot.

From my observations, I offer the following suggestions for site criteria:

- Place nests where they will get early morning sun. Let them face east or south. Insects are cold blooded and so require the heat of the sun to get them up to operating temperature each morning.
- Minimize the exposure to wind. The females carry loads of mud and food that equal a substantial percentage of their body weight. They need every advantage they can get.
- Don't hang the nest block in a tree. It is apt to be shaded there; it swings and it is exposed to the wind. The bees will find your fruit tree if their nest is within several hundred feet. Put their home in the sunniest, most protected place you can find. If you must put the nest block in a tree, at least fix it solidly to the trunk, and in the best position to get maximum sun.
- Locate your bees where you can enjoy them. They are fascinating to watch and they will not bother you.

The wall of your house just low enough to get the morning sun and still be protected by the roof overhang might be just right.

- Hang all of your nesting blocks close together. Remember, these bees are gregarious. They don't want space between themselves and their neighbors. The Orchard Mason wants to live cheek by jowl, so to speak.

- Don't move the nesting blocks around once the bees have emerged. Like the honey bee, the Orchard Mason has a very finely tuned directional sense. If the foraging female leaves on a mission and returns to find that her well meaning gardener has decided she might enjoy the view better from the rose trellis, the confused lady will simply go looking for another home, perhaps a couple of houses down the block.

- Provide moist dirt if you live in an arid climate. You can lay down a small piece of plastic in your garden, shovel dirt into it and then keep it moist with a watering can from time to time. The bees like earth with a specific moisture content. You might want to heap the earth up so that water drains through it. This way the bees can extract masonry materials from the dirt level containing the suitable moisture level.

- Store the filled nesting blocks for the winter in an unheated building or in a dry location under a roof eave. Don't worry about brief freezing temperatures. The bees confront freezes in their natural environment and survive nicely. Remember, these are natives; they are acclimated to the North American weather. If, however, you live in an area with long winter freezes, mortality will increase unless you simulate natural conditions. A bee hibernating deep inside a log, buried under two feet of snow, is insulated from the cold. A bee, hibernating in a four by six beam, exposed on the apple tree in your back yard to three months of sub-zero cold, is going to have a tough job of survival. Use your imagination and good judgment. Try to simulate natural conditions.

- Don't be impatient with the emerging bees. There is not a darned thing that you can do to help them enter this world, nor can you speed them up. Their emergence is entirely controlled by an age-old stimulus response system that is not entirely understood but is surely based on temperature.

Some years the bees emerge in late February, and extend their emergence over a number of weeks. In other years they emerge in early April and just seem to burst out of the holes in a period of days. This seemingly erratic emergence pattern is obviously a response to the weather.

In the remarkably warm Puget Sound winter of 1991-92, the bees began emerging in my yard on February 27th. They continued emerging daily over a long period of time. My observation notes identify March 20th as the first date that I saw a female. This means that males emerged for twenty-three days before a female was identified. The females completed their emergence with more dispatch, but they also came out over at least a ten day period.

In several locations where sunlight was not sufficient, the start was a good deal later. I had several reports from persons using the "pollinators" that I had sold them of nesting bees even as late as August. I am skeptical of those reports but mention them to illustrate that nature will dictate the timing of the bee's cycle.

We must be patient, unlike one friend with a "pollinator" who dug out the mud entrance plugs from the nesting holes with a pipe cleaner and then probed the chambers, thinking to help the poor bees escape their trap. Needless to say the bees did not survive his well-intentioned ministrations.

Rest assured that the bees' emergence will coincide with the blossoming of their food source. Nature has hooked them into the same temperature/sunlight wake up signal. Bees and blossoms are inter-dependent. It could be no other way.

Having said that you can't rush the emergence, you should know that you can delay spring emergence. You simply fool the bees into thinking it is still winter, by putting them into the refrigerator. You might want to do this if you have a late blooming fruit tree and very few early blossoms to hold the bees in your neighborhood. Japanese orchardists have controlled the emergence of *Osmia Cornifrons* in their orchards for many years. They simply refrigerate nesting blocks and warm them up three days before they need bees.

After the eggs are laid and the nesting chambers completed, the bees are subject to serious peril if the nesting blocks are handled roughly. Jarring the nesting cells can result in one-hundred percent mortality of the eggs and larvae. At the earliest stage a sudden jolt can dislodge the egg from the food provision. The dislodged egg dehydrates and dies.

Even after its hatching, the larva can be easily dislodged from its grip on the cell's food. Unable to climb back to a feeding position, it will die.

Through its entire metamorphosis, with the exception of one month just after cocoon spinning, mortality can be caused by rough handling. It is far safer to leave nesting blocks hanging until cool weather in October. By that time, each cell will contain a cocoon in which rests an adult Orchard Mason bee sleeping the long sleep until the coming spring. Rough handling won't bother them now. You can move the filled nesting blocks very gently at any time if you have a reason to do so. You might wish to move them out of the traffic of children, or pets, or to move the blocks under rain protection. If you must move them be gentle, and wait until the blocks are filled, or the bees have stopped working them.

I mentioned earlier the need for a healthful environment in which to propagate these bees. I speak largely of the use of pesticides in the proximity of the Orchard Mason. If you and your immediate neighbors use pesticides between February and late May, you may create a world in which the Orchard Mason, and most other beneficial insects, cannot survive.

While there may be times and places when specific

pesticides must be used, backyard gardeners can have great success with almost no pesticide use.

We have found that we must spray with *Bacillus Thuringensus* in the spring to control the various lepidoptera caterpillars which chomp on our fruit tree leaves. We also spray oil and dormant spray chemicals to control the scab insects, but beyond that we rely on natural controls.

Over recent years we have come to believe that achieving something of a natural balance is indeed reducing insect damage to the flowers, vegetables and fruit in our garden. At the very least we would rather eat around the occasional insect hole in an apple, than think about the toxic threats of a perfect, sprayed fruit.

We believe one of our best allies in the battle against the bugs are the chickadees and violet green swallows that nest in our garden. These two bird species nest very successfully in bird houses in urban gardens.

We have six birdhouses attached to the various buildings on our city lot. Five of them are attached to the house. By midsummer, we have a small flock of immature birds searching for bugs all over the garden.

Each sunny morning the bird bath sounds and looks like a high school swim meet.

Many other bird species trade in our yard: crows, jays, starlings, robins, rosy finches. The reliable attraction is a bird bath made from an old oak wine barrel standing on end. Water drips constantly from the antique brass faucet above into the shallow pool formed by the barrel head, keeping the water always fresh.

All morning every morning there is a line up at the barrel as the birds compete for their turn. I have noticed that if I turn the water off so that it no longer drips, the birds go elsewhere to bathe. They like fresh clean oxygenated water -- and who can blame them?

Pesticides can be devastating to the Orchard Mason or any other bee. However, our friend does have several protective advantages over the honey bee. The honey bee foraging on blossoms sprayed with poison can pick the pesticides up on its body and return to the hive where others will groom her. The intimate lifestyle of the honey bee can spread the toxins from bee to bee throughout the hive.

The solitary nature of *Osmia Lignaria* offers some protection from toxic sprays. If an individual bee is exposed and survives long enough to get back to the nesting site, the toxins will only affect the health of the cell she is working on. Because she has no contact with other bees, she will not spread the poisons carried on her body. Hopefully, those eggs previously laid and sealed in the nesting chamber will survive to emerge the next spring.

The Orchard Mason lives outside its nesting cell for such a short period of time that if you and your neighbors can refrain from spraying toxic materials until after the foraging season ends in late May, you will kill none of your population of bees. By June 1st, the adults have already died and their work is done. The eggs holding next year's population are safe behind their walls of mud.

Chapter 6

PREDATORS AND PARASITES

It seems an immutable law of nature that all creatures are prey for some other species. Our Orchard Mason is no exception. In nature's plan a certain percentage of the population of any species becomes dinner for some other species. This remarkable interdependence in the natural world is brutal, but it seems to work with a marvelous logic.

The ingenious techniques of the predators, and the unique defenses adopted by the preyed-upon are, for me, the most interesting of nature's wonders. The Orchard Mason bee is prey for a number of predators at all stages of its life. At no time in its life cycle is it more vulnerable than when cloistered in the mud walls of the nesting cell.

For ten months and more, the future of the Orchard Mason species depends on the security of those nesting cells. Beyond the physical security of the cell, there are fascinating adaptations of life that assure the survival of the species.

For instance, why does the female Orchard Mason create two-thirds of her babies as males, and lay those male eggs invariably in the front cells of the nesting chamber? Does she realize, through some primal instinct, that the males are only important for one brief act of copulation, and that only a few have to survive until the spring to procreate?

It is the females that assure the survival of the species. They must be protected, so female eggs are laid in the back of the hole. Any predator invading the sanctity of the nesting hole must savage all the males before it gets to the females. Hopefully, spring emergence will occur before the predator eats its way back to the ladies.

Why does the Orchard Mason construct thin walls separating the nesting cells, but brick up a really thick one at the entrance to the hole? How does she know the first wall is the really important line of defense to keep the barbarians at the gate? Such adaptations help reduce bee mortality, but a certain population loss appears inevitable each year. The Orchard Mason simply has too many enemies to escape depredation.

In the world outside the nesting cell, birds are probably the worst danger; robins, magpies, any insect-eating bird will feast on the flying insect. I have observed a pair of red-breasted sapsuckers sitting on a nesting trap picking off the female Orchard Masons as they returned to the nesting holes.

Woodpeckers of many kinds will invade the nesting blocks, looking for succulent larva. I have heard of field mice excavating the nesting holes in search of the hibernating bees.

Depredations by these larger creatures are probably catastrophic when they occur, but they would not be the prime cause of bee mortality. In the natural world, depredation of the nesting cells by their fellow insects takes a greater toll. One of the worst enemies of the Orchard Mason is the *Stelis Montana* bee, a member of the same Megachilid family. Our friend is not even safe from its close relatives. A tiny wasp represents another serious threat. This wasp plants its eggs on the larva of the Orchard Mason. Its larva then consumes the Orchard Mason larva.

The Orchard Mason is at least pestered by, and perhaps damaged by, the tiny pink colored mite that we mentioned in a previous chapter. We will examine its relationship with the bee.

A variety of marauding beetle larvae and other nest associates can take their toll on the bees or their larvae, and finally the bees can suffer mortality from disease and fungal infections.

Despite all these assaults on the population of the Orchard Mason, the bees survive and prosper. Depredation is merely part of the balance that nature has established. The predators and problems seem to control the population but never entirely destroy it. Let's take a closer look at some of these predators. You will want to be able to identify them as you observe your bees.

MITES

Let us first discuss the parasitic mite. Its name is *Chaetodactylus Krombeini Baker*. This tiny creature thrives in nesting cells where the food provision was not completely eaten by the larva. It is pinkish in color, and is most populous in cells where the egg did not hatch for some reason and the entire food provision did not get eaten. There, the whole food hoard is available to nurture the mites and a teeming population results.

There is some question as to whether the mite kills the egg thereby freeing all that food for its progeny, or if it simply coexists with the bee, sharing the cell's provisions. Karl Krombein, in his 1962 paper, "Biological Notes on *Chaetodactylus Krombeini Baker*", unequivocally states he has "observed adult mites attacking and feeding on the bee egg and consuming its fluids." He was working with the Eastern Orchard Mason, at Plummers Island, Maryland. Torchio, on the other hand, has tried repeatedly to get the mite to attack the eggs of the Western bee, without success. In a personal communication, he has told me he cannot state that the mite kills the western bee.

You have already read that the mites cluster on the thorax of the newly emerged bee. It is clear that the mite clambers aboard the emerging bee sometime between when the bee emerges from the cocoon and the time that it leaves the nesting hole.

Periodically, I split open nesting blocks to examine the cells and their contents. Those examinations indicate that the mites don't live inside the cocoon. They live inside the nesting cell, scavenging any unused pollen-nectar supplies. Small numbers of them are found in nesting cells containing a healthy cocoon but the large numbers are to be found in cells where for some reason the egg did not hatch and the entire food provision is available to them.

Those heavily Infested cells are identified by the yellow food provision that becomes loose and granulated by action of the feeding mites. The mites seem to be constantly moving through the loose mass of food, further churning it to a fluffy pile. The cell will be entirely filled with this fluffy mass.

It appears common to find an infested cell positively teeming with mites, yet the cells both in front and behind will be unaffected. Just as common, when excavating nesting holes, is to find a cell with the food provision intact in a solid waxy lump of pollen and nectar. There will be no sign of the mites. For one reason or another, the egg failed to hatch and the unused food provision remains in its solid original condition.

I deduce from these observations that the mites cannot pass through cell walls. They must be present as eggs or adults on the female bees as they prepare the nesting cell in the spring. They then apparently hatch or drop off in the cell to eat up food left by the larva.

It is also possible that the mites ride into the cell on the back of the female bee, drop off in a nesting cell, and proceed to kill the egg, thereby guaranteeing a plentiful food supply for the offspring that will soon develop.

The mites are evident in cells in October and seemingly live in the cell all winter to emerge in the spring riding the back of the bee. Are they seeking a ride to new regions? Or are they laying eggs on the bee to assure that their progeny will have a future? Or perhaps they are riding the bee so that they can jump off in the new nesting hole that the females will be provisioning. Do they begin feeding on the new food provision? I don't know and have been unable to find the answers.

The emerging bees are apparently infested as they crawl

through the long hole and its various nesting cells. When the emerging bees break down the mud cell walls, the mites are free to travel from their infested cell to all the other cells and to clamber aboard the backs of the bees passing by on their way to the outside world.

The bees seem to be successful in scraping the mites off in a day or two. Perhaps the mites "bail out" over some tempting target to which the bees have flown them. At any rate, in a few days the bees are shiny, blue-black and appear to be mite free.

Little is known about the life history of this mite and its relationship with its host. It is apparently not detrimental to the success of the bee unless mite concentrations become so heavy that damage to the bee's wings result or unless the mites kill the bee eggs as mentioned before.

Dickman, in "Orchard Bee" says you can control mites by removing bee cocoons from the nesting holes, immersing them, for 5 or 10 minutes in a solution of water and 5% bleach. The cocoons are waterproof, thus the bees are not harmed. Any mites on the cocoons are killed. Then you must replace the cocoons into a nesting hole, or a straw, finally plugging the entrance with a small wad of cotton.

The writer suggested the importance of aligning all replaced cocoons, "nipple" end toward the entrance. The head of the bee faces the slight protuberance at one end of the cocoon. I guess he wants to avoid starting the bee in the wrong direction during spring emergence.

MONODONTOMERUS WASPS

These tiny Chalcid wasps are the most serious parasite of

the Orchard Mason Bee. The wasps invade the bee nesting cells only after the cocoon is spun. They touch their sensitive antennae to the wood of the nesting block to detect the movements of the larvae or pupae within the cell. When they detect movement, they insert their ovipositor through the wood, into the cell, through the cocoon to lay an egg upon the larva or pupa within.

The egg hatches and the wasp larva, now comfortably within the chamber of the bee, slowly eats away the bee larva - a grisly but successful way to make a living indeed.

The wasp larva, having consumed its host, hibernates, and emerges from the commandeered bee nesting hole the next year, just in time to assault another generation of Orchard Mason cocoons. These wasps are most damaging when Orchard Mason eggs are laid in thin walled nesting holes such as paper straws or hollow plant stems. The ovipositor is capable of easily piercing the thin walls and planting the egg on the resident pupa. Dr. Torchio tells me that indeed the *Monodontomerus* can penetrate wood up to 3/4s the length of its long ovipositor.

If you are able to get access to a microscope as mentioned in the final chapter, make every effort to capture and look at one of these miniature wasps. They are incredibly beautiful and graceful. Be sure to note the ovipositor sheath which protrudes from their rear. You will see that it is merely support for the ovipositor, which lies folded up under the wasp's abdomen. With a pin try to fold out the ovipositor. You will not believe its length. The thought that a structure small and strong enough to pierce wood and pass an egg through it, could also be foldable, staggers my imagination.

Watch for this little killer cruising your nesting blocks in early June.

STELIS MONTANA

This bee predator is a member of the same Megachilidae family that the Orchard Mason belongs to. It victimizes a number of the *Megachilid* bees, including *Osmia Californica*, and *Osmia Montana* mentioned previously.

The *Stelis* female patrols the Orchard Mason nesting site, flying ten to fifteen centimeters in front of the nesting blocks. Finding a likely nesting hole that has not yet been completed, she lands at the entrance and directs her sensitive antennae into the hole. Is she checking for a protective mother Orchard Mason, or is she somehow learning whether or not the nesting cell is still open?

If her inspection is favorable, she enters and deposits her egg in the partially prepared food provision. She always takes care to lay her egg at some distance from the spot that the Orchard Mason will eventually lay her egg.

The *Stelis* initiates flight at a warmer temperature than the Orchard Mason. The marauding female is usually on patrol at least an hour after the Orchard Mason has started work. By the time she is at work, our Orchard Mason mother has had time to gather enough food to start another cell, but not to seal it up - just what the female *Stelis* wants. Sometimes several *Stelis* females will each lay an egg in the same cell. Thus there will be more than one parasite in the cell when it is sealed.

The hardworking female Orchard Mason returns with a fresh load of nesting materials, not knowing that there is one or several intruders in her nest who will eventually slay her offspring. She completes the nest cell and seals it up, unaware of the danger.

Stelis eggs are small in relation to the host egg: approximately 2 mm rather than the 3 to 3.4 mm of the Orchard Mason. They are nearly straight or slightly curved. In about five days they enter the embryo stage, then the larval stage, and by the time they have progressed to the fifth larval stage they are mobile. The first act of the *Stelis* larva is to kill its competition. If there is another *Stelis* larva in the cell, it is attacked and killed but not eaten.

Attention is then turned to the large Orchard Mason larva. It too is assassinated, but unlike the dead *Stelis* larva, this meal is tempting. The juices are sucked from the punctured carcass by the surviving *Stelis*. When the larva has been consumed, baby *Stelis* now turns to the remaining pollen and nectar supply. After eating its fill the *Stelis* larva spins its cocoon. There it will complete its maturing process, sleep away the winter, and re-emerge in the following spring.

The *Stelis* spends the winter in a pre-pupal stage, molting into the Pupa during the emergence stage of the Orchard Mason. It rapidly completes its metamorphosis, and by the time the Orchard Mason is at the peak of its egg-laying activity, the adult *Stelis Montana* chews out of its cocoon and emerges. Three or four days later, it has mated, and is patrolling the nesting sites, ready to do its dirty deed to another generation of Orchard Masons.

Stelis Montana sounds like a deadly threat that would destroy every last *Osmia* bee, but nature is more clever than that.

Remember, *Stelis* emerges after our Orchard Mason is at the peak of egg laying, three or four more days are spent feeding and mating, and by the time the *Stelis* female starts her deadly work, there are already lots of nesting cells completed, safe from her depredations.

Even better, most of the female eggs have been laid in those early cells. The *Stelis* predator kills a lot of bees but does not really damage the population of *Osmia* bees too badly because it kills mostly the males. Fortunately, its larvae do not invade adjoining cells. They cannot break through the mud walls.

Torchio's study shows that of cells invaded by *Stelis*, 48.0% were the outermost cell. 20.9% in the 2nd cell and 15.1% in the 3rd cell. That means 84% of all *Stelis* damage was done to the outermost three cells. Nature has sacrificed the males by having the mother bee lay male eggs in the first cells of the nesting hole. The species survives.

TRICRANIA STANSBURYI

This beetle is a parasite of several megachilid bees throughout western North America. A second species of *Tricrania* is widely distributed in the eastern United States and is a parasite of at least three bees on that side of the country. The adult beetles of both species are similar in appearance. They are black, with blood red wing-covers, and measure six to ten millimeters in length. Strangely, the eastern species is flightless, while the western insect has well developed wings.

This beetle has been a known predator of the Orchard

Mason for many years. Because its depredations were minor in all previous studies, the beetle's biology has not been extensively studied. However, in 1989 and 1990 the rates of its parasitism rose in one location in Utah from the expected one or two percent, to fourteen percent and thirty three percent, respectively. A closer look at this creature was justified.

The *Tricrania Stansburyi* life cycle begins in the nesting cell of a host bee. The adult beetles emerge in the spring with the emerging bees, and immediately, courtship and mating begin. A female will frequently mate with several males, but soon it loses interest and flies off to look for a plant to lay its cluster of eggs upon.

Two or three days after emergence, *T. stansburyi* lays its cluster of eggs on certain, selected plant species. Each female lays an average of four hundred eggs, bound together by a sticky substance secreted by the beetle. On the seventh or eighth day after being laid, the rapidly developing eggs split open to release the triungulin, or first larval stage.

The triungulins look a little like miniature earwigs with pinchers on the front rather than behind. The larvae are long and thin with prominent mandibles and a forked tail. They are mobile, with short legs, and are attracted toward light so that they crawl upward toward the sun. They climb and climb on their pre-selected plant, until they reach the top level, the blossom. There they arch their backs upward and wave their mandibles whenever a stranger passes by.

You have already guessed the rest of the story, I suspect. A foraging bee lands on the blossom and brushes its hairy leg over the waiting triungulin. Snap! The mandibles close over a fine hair on the bees leg, and the triungulin hangs on for the ride of its life. The unsuspecting bee flies back to the nesting cell with its load of pollen and nectar. As soon as it enters the cell, the triungulin lets go of the bee hair.

The bee, frequently an Orchard Mason, seals up the nesting cell not knowing that her recently laid egg is doomed. The triungulin gets right to work. If by chance several triungulins rode in on the same bee, mortal combat ensues immediately. The victor then attacks the freshly laid egg, piercing it with its recurved mandibles. For several days it feasts on the juices of the egg until the egg case is empty. Then the triungulin turns to the pollen and nectar supply.

Strangely enough, the triungulin cannot survive in a cell with only pollen and nectar and no egg. It apparently must eat the egg to get itself to the next stage, at which it can eat the pollen and nectar. Additionally, two triungulins introduced to a cell with no egg, pollen, or nectar will not initiate combat but will die of starvation.

The victorious triungulin, having dined on the egg and secure in the bee cell surrounded by rich pollen and nectar, need only eat and grow and evolve. Soon, its metamorphosis is complete, and like the host bee, it enters a state of torpor. All fall and winter it sleeps in the cell awaiting the spring and the renewal of its life cycle.

This story must end by reporting that the thirty five percent parasitism rate reported earlier was explained by Philip Torchio's study: 1989 and 1990 were drought years in Utah. The wild flowers favored by the Orchard Mason, in the particular desert canyon studied, did not bloom well. The bees were forced to forage on a secondary flower choice, one favored by *T. Stansburyi*. Had they been able to use their traditional flowers, the parasitism rate probably would have stayed at one percent.

OTHER ENEMIES

Among the other creatures that victimize the Orchard Mason is a cocoon wasp (*leucospis*) and a carpet beetle (*Anthrenus verbasci*) that is attracted to opened cells and old nests. The larvae of the carpet beetle are capable of digging through the mud dividing walls.

There is also a large yellow and black solitary wasp that competes with the Orchard Mason for nesting holes. They feed on small caterpillars and are actually a beneficial insect, but they will damage the *Osmia Lignaria* cells as they emerge by tearing down the walls.

The Orchard Mason shares one health threat with the honey bee, chalkbrood. This fungal affliction was first reported in Europe in 1944. It was found in the New World by Baker and Torchio in 1968. By 1974 thirty-five states had confirmed its presence. Chalkbrood has become a major problem for commercial honey bee producers. The fungus, *Ascosphaera torchioi*, afflicts both the honey bee and the Orchard Mason.

You can recognize chalkbrood if you open a nesting hole and find cells containing partially completed cocoons that are dry and brittle and contain round black fungal organisms. Apparently chalkbrood only affects one to two percent of healthy Orchard Mason colonies and is not considered the threat that it poses to honey bee colonies.

Alarming as all these predators, parasites, and diseases seem, they are all part of the marvelous balance that nature has established. These predators control the population but never entirely destroy it.

Our advice would be to watch with curiosity the depredations of these various insects. Don't interfere unless your Orchard Masons seem to be seriously threatened.

You can prevent depredation with some ingenious techniques. For instance If you cover filled nesting blocks with an old nylon stocking, the *Monodontomerus* wasps can't get close enough to attack. If you remove your nesting blocks to an unheated outbuilding in the fall, the woodpeckers and magpies won't excavate the holes for winter protein.

The Orchard Mason has survived in North America for millions of years. Have faith that it will continue to thrive in the face of its enemies and make a home in your back yard.

Chapter 7

FUN WITH BEES

If you decide to propagate the Orchard Mason for yourself, beware! You will be opening the door to a new world of activity. Your curiosity may lead you to all sorts of projects and interests that you had never anticipated. Some of your friends might begin to discuss you behind your back. Even your family may begin to apologize for your strange behavior.

I speak from experience, but without apology, for I have found great joy in my fascination with the Orchard Mason. Perhaps you will wish to try some of the following tips on having fun with your bees.

MAKE AN OBSERVATION BOX

Last spring I made an observation box which has allowed me to see in great detail and clarity the completed nesting cell. There is the food pile, pollen and nectar piled in a golden hoard. Implanted in it is the shimmering egg. I have watched the egg become a larva, the larva eat the food and finally spin itself into its silken cocoon.

I have seen the carefully constructed masonry walls, and the thick entrance plug. Hopefully, in the spring, I will watch the bees awaken and work their way out to the sunshine.

The observation block is a wonderful tool to excite children about nature. Children and adults alike look intently at the orderly cell construction and the life within, and they begin to understand what you have been telling them about the life history of the Orchard Mason. If a picture is worth a thousand words, peering into the secret chamber of the bee nest is even better. Some of the notes of my observation file might illustrate.

June 24th, 1992: Today the #1 larva spun its cocoon. In twenty four hours it is completely encased and the cocoon is attached to the sides of the chamber. The nipple facing the anterior end is prominent and obvious. Pretty amazing.

June 27th, 1992: This day the larva in cell #2 began to spin. With one end immobile, the anterior end extended and traced the outline of the cocoon, spinning with invisible threads. Only after some time did the accumulation of threads begin to obscure the outline of the larva. The next morning the larva was encased and not visible behind the light colored cocoon. I presume the spinning continues for some time inside an ever thickening cocoon. The cocoon darkens in color over a period of several days, either because of the increasing thickness or because the threads are exposed to the atmosphere.

Now the long nine month wait as the metamorphosis continues behind that opaque brown cocoon. I expect to watch in the spring, as the wakened bees answer natures summons to the daylight.

All this is possible because the bees will lay eggs in a glass tube. Here is how you can do it.

Clamp two perfectly flat pieces of wood tightly together. Then drill directly down the joint line separating the blocks, creating a hole which is one half drilled in each block of wood. Insert into each hole a small glass tube with an inside diameter of seven millimeters, or 5/16ths of an inch. Secure the tube to one block with a spot of epoxy, or a thin copper wire. Plug one end of each tube with a piece of wooden dowel. The tubes must be tightly plugged at the back. If a predator can get in the back, the bees won't use the tubes. Now all that you need to do is attach two small hinges, and some sort of a closing latch. A hook and eye will do.

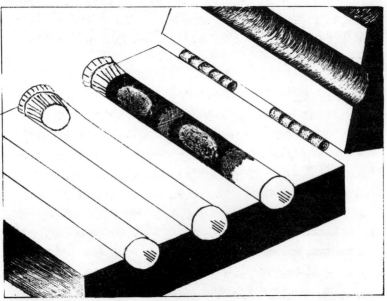

Now you are ready to hang the observation block with your other nesting blocks in the hope that a bee will use it. I would encourage you to have the observation block ready at the very first of the season when you hang the others. Because this idea came mid-season last year, I installed it when the nesting patterns of the females were already well established. The bees only constructed two nest cells in one of the three tubes in my box.

KEEP AN OBSERVATION JOURNAL

There is much to be learned about the Orchard Mason bee and its propagation. I strongly suggest that you take observation notes as you watch this fascinating creature. Doing so will increase your enjoyment, heighten your powers of observation, and teach you a great deal about the bee as the years go on.

Last year I began recording observations on my computer when the mood struck. I have found those notes to be valuable in review. You might enjoy excerpts from some early notes from last spring.

March 4th, 1992: *The bees are emerging rapidly this morning. I stand at the blocks and watch their heads first appear at the holes, then widen their hole in the mud wall, and finally squeeze through to freedom. It's pretty exciting as several can be seen at once. When they get out many of them drop to the ground and groom their wings. Then they fly off. Already some return to the breeding blocks and even re-enter the holes for a brief period as though they recognize the holes as home base.*

At emergence the bees have a russet patch of what looks like thick hair on the back of their thorax. It will be interesting to see if that disappears with age. The bees seem to all be males. Not shiny at emergence. Several that have flown back to the blocks are quite shiny.

March 22, 1992: *The bees at emergence have a russet red, granular substance all over their thorax. They rub it off after a day or two and thereafter are bright and shiny. I first thought it was a hair covering of some sort, but the last few days I've been thinking it might be a parasite. A mite perhaps, because around several of the nesting holes I see a mass of similar colored substance which in heavy concentrations seems to move.*

Surely what I am seeing on the blocks is a mite of some sort. Can it be possible that they share the nesting hole with some sort of beneficial mite that covers their thorax at emergence? I called an acquaintance in Bellevue to test my theory. He would have none of it, assuring me that the red covering was to keep them from freezing in the nesting hole.

<u>March 23, 1992</u>: About three days ago I began seeing the females. Prior to that time I had been intently looking at males and trying to see a female. Once you see the females there is no mistaking them. They are MUCH larger; they buzz when they fly with a loud and bee-like sound. Their antennae are about half as long as the males'. They are already laying eggs and building nesting chambers. Their flights are purposeful - frequently direct to the hole, in, out and on about their business, A great contrast to the males which flit from place to place with lots of frantic circling and chasing. The males are obviously obsessed with mating. They fly up and "hit" other males sitting for a moment in the sun, then fly away to "hit" another. Apparently they are looking for females. When they see a black insect they dive at it and "hit" it but, I assume, immediately realize it is of the wrong sex or species and so bounce off and look for another. Occasionally they mount another male, only proving that sexual deviation is not peculiar to the human species.

<u>March 24, 1992</u>: Today I made a rather exciting discovery. The russet, red coating on the thorax of the newly emerging bee is in fact a mass of tiny microscopic

mites of some kind.

I had placed a newly emerged female in the observation box last night. I was interested in how long it would take her to scrape off the red coating, and how long before her wings would open and she would take flight.

At lights out last night the coating was covering the back of her thorax. This morning, before she stirred from the crevice she had spent the night in, and before she became active, I checked her.

Some of the red substance had moved to the top of her wings. Aha! My earlier suspicion that the red stuff was in fact a living organism took on more credence.

Later this afternoon I found a newly hatched female on the courtyard bricks. She had been slightly mangled by a passing shoe. Her ardent suitor had been squished. I picked her up and took her to the shop, found my tiny penlight magnifier and scraped some red stuff onto a piece of white paper. It was soon apparent that I was dealing with something alive. The tiny gob of red stuff, separated into tiny, barely visible specks that moved across the paper.

Faced with a rampant curiosity, I went to visit a neighbor who owns an excellent microscope. We soon had the mystery solved. The back of the bee was infested with a mass of ugly little pink mites, all moving legs and what looked like antenna or cilia. When placed on paper they crawled rather rapidly around. An ugly mass of bug to say the least.

Now to find out what they are. I conclude that they are some sort of symbiotic insect which shares the bee's nesting chamber and does some service for him in return for a benefit received. What that benefit might be I have no idea. For the present I will assume they are not harmful. My Bellevue acquaintance has them on his bees in Bellevue. I would bet all Orchard Mason Bees have them. It will be fascinating to learn just what they are and what they do for the relationship.

Emergence: not a lot of new holes opened today. I think only two, but I saw at least four new females. All of them on the ground, with immature wings (I was wrong the wings were mature but damp), being mated by an eager male. In one case the male was also covered with the red mites. Is it possible that the male and female emerged from the same or neighboring holes and immediately began copulating upon getting outdoors? As aggressive and desperate as the older males appear, one would think they would find and mount the females first.

The females at emergence, are slow, with underdeveloped-appearing wings, and laden with mites. Most of them seem to fall to the ground to get limbered up and cleaned off. only to be found and mounted by a lusty male. It may be nature's way of getting them bred before they are too mobile. The females must grow after emergence, as the ones I have been seeing on the ground are a good bit smaller than the great, fat-bellied ladies that are so busily working the nesting blocks. (I later learned that adult insects don't grow. These bees were damp from the cocoon. As their hairs dried they appeared larger)

March 29th, 1992: The spring weather continues warm and sunny. Each day for the last six or seven days I have seen new females emerging. They frequently come out of a hole and are immediately mounted by a hovering male. Then another male piles on, and the weight of two males causes the female to let go, and all three of them fall to the ground where the copulation continues.

In one instance I saw a female's head emerge. Immediately a male pounced, trying to pull her out of the hole. She pulled out of his grasp and retreated backwards into the hole. The male followed her in. After a bit the female emerged and right behind her was the male who instantly mounted her as they got out of the hole. He had crawled past her, turned in the hole, and drove her out with his attentions.

There continues to be a significant size differential in bees both male and female. There are several males so small that they appear to be a separate miniature species. They are half the size of the average male but appear to be Orchard Masons in every respect. Some of the females are really huge, with nicely rounded abdomens and a healthy bee buzz when flying. The females, when they emerge are noticeably smaller than those working the nests. I would surmise that they grow in all dimensions upon emergence. Surely being bred and filling with eggs has a lot to do with the growth. (Wrong again. See the note in parentheses in the Emergence paragraph above. Observations can be misleading)

April 5th, 1992: The weather has remained at record warm temperatures until yesterday. This morning at 10:30 A.M. the thermometer on the garden house shows fifty-five degrees. The females are working, although at a slower pace than on a good day. Numbers of them are visible at the hole entrances as though they are waiting for a little better temperature, or they are soaking up enough heat from the wood block for their next foray after nesting materials.

The blocks continue to fill at a satisfying pace. I have one block drilled with 1/4 inch holes and just a dozen 5/16 inch holes. The smaller holes have definitely filled faster than the larger holes, although when watching the bees I have the sense that the same proportion of bees are going to each sized hole.

Perhaps it is simply easier for them to fill the smaller holes because of the smaller volume and so they do it more rapidly.

Whether or not the percentage of females is higher in the larger holes, one compelling reason to switch to 5/16 inch is to avoid expanding wood fibers from sealing up the entrance to the 1/4 inch hole. It seems that if the wood is fairly soft, the fibers expand with outdoor moisture.

Another factor surely must be the sharpness of the drill bit. If it is dull some fibers will be bent and not cut. When moistened they straighten and plug the hole. A very sharp brad point drill bit will be the best. All things considered I am convinced that the 5/16ths hole is the best bet.

April 6th, 1992: Today I had big news. I again called Dr. Dan Meyer at the WSU office at Prosser. He assured me that the mites were no big deal. A common and symbiotic rider on Orchard Mason Bees. They are not a problem unless they get so thick that they can stunt the bees wings. I guess I have no problem after all, for which I am grateful and relieved."

I hope the foregoing sample of my "Observation Notes" hints at the excitement of learning that I have so enjoyed with these bees. There is much that science doesn't yet understand in the life and nature of these creatures. Your experiences, duly recorded in notes of some kind, could make a contribution to man's understanding of the wild bees. At the very least such notes provide a record of when things occurred in the past, so you can have some idea of what to expect in the future.

BEE WATCHING

Observation of these busy little pollinators is a great pleasure for children. There is enough activity at the nesting blocks that my active pre-school grandchildren will sit on my knee watching for amazing periods of time. A bee's foraging round trip is of short duration. I sometimes place a pencil mark below a hole that is being used, and we watch and wait for that particular bee to return.

There is great excitement when the bee returns to her hole. Then it is important to see if we can spot the yellow pollen in the scopa on the bottom of her abdomen. If she is bearing pollen, we can usually see her yellow bottom just as she scuttles into the hole.

Perhaps the greatest fun for kids is counting the nesting females at night. Each evening when the temperature cools below the bee's operating level, the females crawl into the nesting hole they have been working at. The children find it fascinating to wait until dark, and then visit the nesting holes with a flashlight. If you shine the light directly down the hole, your eye is greeted with a shiny black abdomen reflecting the light back to you.

It is not only great fun to count the bees, but it is valuable information for serious bee propagators. You can learn how many nesters you have, when their population peaks and when they begin to die off - Kind of a military muster of troop strength.

Children respond well to learning about these bees. The bees seem to stimulate that wonderful curiosity that children possess in such abundance. The secret to opening their minds to the wonder of nature is to make discovery fun. Use your Orchard Mason colony to catch a child's curiosity.

Let the children watch the bees emerge. Remember, most of the bees emerge from 10 to 11 in the morning. You may find yourself having to explain about "the birds and the bees" but what better time and place? Don't make a big deal out of it. Treat the subject matter-of-factly and simply. The children will handle it just fine.

Observe together the insects feeding at a flowering shrub. As you look for your Orchard Masons you will see many other insects. Now you can point out the difference between flies and bees. Remember? Bees have four wings, flies but two. You will see honey bees; tell them about the pollen baskets on honey bee legs. You can watch the several varieties of bumble bees. Do the kids know that most "bumbles" nest in the ground?

Explain pollination in a simple way and then go to see if you can find the Orchard Masons on the apple blossoms. Brush some pollen on the child's hand from a ripe blossom. Tell them about nectar and explain that bees drink it, partly to regurgitate it later to mix with their collected pollen.

BEE COLLECTION

You might want to encourage a child to collect, identify and mount insects of a certain group. A collection of bees could be an exciting summer project for both a child or grandchild, and yourself.

A beginning can be had by catching bees in a jar. A small flat paper box with plastic foam cut for the bottom will hold your collection. The small pins that come with new men's shirts are quite adequate for displaying your bees. Killing the insects may be the most difficult part of the project. You can do this very efficiently by purchasing automotive starting fluid (ether) in a pressurized can. Any automotive store stocks ether because it is an extremely flammable gas. Sprayed into a reluctant carburetor, it will bring an engine roaring to life. It has the opposite effect on insects, and for that matter, on humans, so handle it with care.

A quick shot of ether under the lid of a quickly opened jar, will render the bees ready for display almost immediately. Pin the bees through the thorax, mount them on the foam bottom of your box, and begin the fun of identifying them.

If you allow the kids to participate at their own pace, they will share your pleasure in insects in general, and the Orchard Mason in particular. If you make the experience fun and interesting you may kindle a lifelong appreciation for nature that will bring the child great satisfaction and joy. One never knows; you may inspire the twenty first century's greatest naturalist.

BORROW A MICROSCOPE

If you have access to a reasonably good microscope, you are in for an afternoon of fun and wonderment. Put a dead Orchard Mason under the lens and focus on nature's incredible design. Now you can see the pollen carrying scopa for yourself. Look at the twin horns on the face of the female western Orchard Mason. If they point downward, you will be looking at her eastern cousin.

Can you see the delicate structure of the framework in her wings? Were you aware that bees have tiny hairs on their wings? Now check the bee over for mites. If she is carrying any, they will probably be clinging to hairs near where the wings connect to the thorax. Look for the true eyes, the three tiny smooth bumps on the forehead. Did you know that bees have two different kinds of eyes?

If you can find a bee that has just emerged with the red mites covering the thorax, get the bee under the microscope and look at that mass of mites. It may make your skin crawl, but it is fascinating.

I think nothing will so open the eyes of a child as their first look at the incredible architecture of an insect, magnified. Be sure you give the children in your life the experience.

USE YOUR IMAGINATION

There are many more interesting ways to exploit your experience with the Orchard Mason, and to share its wonders with those around you. Enjoy your experience with this benevolent and beneficial creature. I hope that you have shared my pleasure in learning about them, and that you will be inspired to introduce the Orchard Mason bee to your back yard.

Addendum to 2nd Printing 1994

My observations indicate that while the bees will build nesting cells in the holes they have just emerged from, they greatly prefer a clean fresh hole. You will have the best success by providing a new nesting block each year. You can keep two sets of nesting blocks and use them in alternate years. Each year when you are sure all females have emerged, remove the old blocks, redrill and cleanse them with a clorox solution.

If you store hibernating bees in the refrigerator keep them from dehydrating by putting the nesting block in a paper bag along with a moistened paper towel. Remoisten monthly.

REFERENCES

Joel K. Phillips and E.C. Klostermeyer. 1976. Nesting behavior of *Osmia Lignaria Propinqua Cresson*. Journal of the Kansas Entomological Society. 51(1) 1978. pp 91-108

Philip F. Torchio. 1976. Use of *Osmia Lignaria* Say as a pollinator in an apple and prune orchard. Journal of the Kansas Entomological Society. 49:475-482

Philip F. Torchio. 1991. Use of *Osmia Lignaria Propinqua* as a mobile pollinator of Orchard crops. Environ. Entomol. 20(2):590-596

Philip F. Torchio. 1985 Field experiments with the pollinator species *Osmia Lignaria Propinqua Cresson*, in apple orchards; Journal of the Kansas Entomological Society 58(3),1985, pp448-464

Philip F. Torchio, 1987. Use of non-honey bee species as pollinators of crops. Entomological Society of Ontario. 118.1987 pp111-124

Philip F. Torchio. 1989. In-nest Biologies and Development of Immature Stages of three *Osmia* Species. Ann.Entomol. Soc. Am. 82(5):599-615(1989)

Philip F. Torchio. 1989. Biology, Immature Development, and adaptive Behavior of *Stelis Montana*, A Cleptoparasite of *Osmia*. Ann Entomol. Soc. Am 82(5):616- 632(1989)

Philip F. Torchio. 1992. Effects of Spore Dosage and Temperature on Pathogenic Expressions of Chalkbrood Syndrome Caused by *Ascosphaera torchioi* within Larvae of *Osmia lignaria propinqua* Environ. Entomol.21(5):1086-1091 (1992)

Karl V. Krombein. 1962, Biological Notes on *Chaetodactylus Krombeini Baker*, a Parasitic Mite of the

Megachilid Bee, *Osmia Lignaria Say.* Proc. Biol. Soc. Wash,. Vol. 75 pp 237-250 (1962)

Philip F. Torchio and J. Bosch, 1992 Biology of Tricrania Stansburyi, a Meloid Beetle Cleptoparasite of the bee Osmia Lignaria Propinqua (Hymenoptera: Megachilidae. Ann. Entomol. Soc. Am 85(6): 713-721 (1992)

Philip F. Torchio: Personal correspondence during 1992.

Washington State University. "Orchard Mason Bee" Extension Service Bulletin 0922. July 1981.

United States Department of Agriculture. Insects, the Yearbook of Agriculture. 1952.

The Xerces Society, Fall 1991 vol. "Wings" pp.4-13

Insects of Western North America. E.O. Essig. The MacMillan Company, 1926

Greg Dickman, "Orchard Bees", Orchard Bees, Auburn, Indiana. Orchard Bees

ABOUT THE AUTHOR

Brian L. Griffin was born in Bellingham, Washington in 1932. He is a graduate of Whitman College with a degree in English literature. A childhood spent exploring the tide pools and forests of the San Juan Islands whetted his curiosity about natural things. Years spent afield hiking and hunting sharpened his powers of observation, and finally an inspiring natural history teacher at Whitman College, Arthur Remple, focused his interest and fueled his curiosity further.

Griffin has spent a long career in business, but has always found time to observe and enjoy nature. For the last six years he has propagated Orchard Mason bees. Retired now, this book is a recitation of his experiences with, and study of the Orchard Mason bee.

He still resides in Bellingham, Washington where he is working on his next book, "The Fruit Tree Espalier"

ABOUT THE ILLUSTRATOR

Sharon Smith has been observing and drawing nature for over 20 years. She graduated from the University of California at Santa Barbara, majoring in Biology and Art, and is a member of the Guild of Natural Science Illustrators.

Sharon's love of nature and rural life brought her to the Pacific Northwest, where she lives deep in the woods beside the Nooksack River.

Previously, she has illustrated children's picture books, a tide pool guidebook, and private commissions. Sharon is presently writing and illustrating a collection of stories about the forest wildlife around her home.

"Field Notes"

"Field Notes"